W9-AWL-425

Playing Hardball

by
Lucy Jane Bledsoe

GLOBE FEARON EDUCATIONAL PUBLISHER
Upper Saddle River, New Jersey
www.globefearon.com

Project Editor: Brian Hawkes
Editorial Assistants: Jennifer Keezer, Jenna Thorsland
Art Supervision: Sharon Ferguson
Production Editor: Regina McAloney
Electronic Page Production: José Lopéz
Manufacturing Supervisor: Mark Cirillo
Cover Design: Sharon Ferguson
Illustrator: Ron Bell/SiI. International

Printed in the United States of America
2 3 4 5 6 7 8 9 10 03 02 01 00

ISBN 0-130-23283-1

GLOBE FEARON EDUCATIONAL PUBLISHER
Upper Saddle River, New Jersey
www.globefearon.com

Contents

1. Forget the Baseball Team

Coach comes up to me in the hall like he does all the time. He says, "Give up that job, Will. You know you can come back on the team."

I look away.

"Will Cruz, hear me out. No one can hit the ball like you do. We are on our way to the championship game. With you and Mack playing, we have it in the bag."

I keep looking away.

"What's the problem?" Coach says. "Just say OK."

"Because," I say, "I have a job. I need the money. I have to work after school."

I played on the baseball team for about 10 weeks. Then I stopped after finding work. I need the job. I can't play baseball.

Coach looks down the hall. He is mad. Then he looks back at me. "Will," he says, "you're 17. After this, there is no more baseball. Believe me, you have time to work and make money after school is out."

I don't talk back to Coach. What more can I say? I know what Dad thinks. Dad says, "You have to start making your own way some time. This is a good time to get started."

Coach looks at me hard. This time he looks at me like he thinks I'm lost. No good. Then he walks away.

I feel like throwing up. I feel bad. I want to play baseball **and** keep my job. It's a good job. I looked and looked and looked for a job. It's hard for kids to get good ones. I'm making a lot of money. I **have** to keep the job.

But I know if the team makes it to the championship game, I'll feel bad. I want to play on the team. But it looks like the team will go to that game without me.

I just have to forget baseball. Baseball is for kids. I have bigger ideas to think about. Mrs. Hall, the principal, says I can go to college. She says my schoolwork is good. That is what Mom wants. Mom says I have to make money for college.

But then what does Mrs. Hall or Mom know? They just like to tell me what to do. They make me mad. What do they know?

Just then Mack Day walks up. He is about to go work out with the baseball team. "What's going on, Will?"

"Not a lot," I say, wanting him to get out of my way. He is my good friend. But I don't like seeing him on his way to the baseball field.

"Listen, Will," he says. "I know how you feel about baseball. I think you should play. You and me, we can take this team all the way to the championship."

"I have to go," I say, walking away. "See you."

"Lighten up, man!" Mack calls after me. "Forget that job! What do you need all that money for? I'll give you $10 a week!"

I don't look back, but I give him a little wave. "Forget baseball," I say. But no one hears me.

"Will," Coach says, "you're 17. After this, there is no more baseball."

2. Finding Out About the Ramoses

I race my mountain bike to my job. I work in a shop called Mountain Works. We sell backpacks, sleeping bags, and mountain bikes. Dan and Kay Ramos own Mountain Works. They are my bosses.

I put my bike in the back of the shop. When I walk into the shop, Dan Ramos starts in on me. "What's your problem? I wanted you to put the backpacks by the wall with the window."

"Sorry," I say. "I'll put them by the wall."

"Forget it," he says. "I'm going to paint that wall. Just put the backpacks over there."

What is his problem? One idea, one day, the next day, another idea. Is this going to be a bad day? I get to work with the backpacks. I don't like Dan Ramos a lot. He is on me all the time. But I work hard because the money is good. I try not to make him mad.

"Dan?" Kay Ramos calls from the back of the shop. "A call for you."

I keep working with the backpacks. But as I go by the back of the shop, I hear Dan Ramos say, "I have him. I'll keep him working. He makes $120 a week. Where will he go?" Then I hear Dan Ramos laugh. "Not a problem," he says. Then he stops talking. The call is over.

He is talking about me! Who is he talking to? My mom? My dad? I don't think they ever call Dan Ramos.

He comes out of the back.

"Do you know that kid Mack Day?" he asks me.

"I know him."

"Good ballplayer, I hear."

What does Dan Ramos want to know about Mack for? "He is good in the field," I say, "and he can really hit."

Dan Ramos smiles. Then he says, "What are you looking at? You have a lot to do. Get at it."

"Sorry," I say, but I want to hit him. "What do you want me to do next?"

"Put some of the new sleeping bags in the

window. Make it look good. After that, I want you to paint the back of the shop."

I look at the time. I don't have time to paint the back of the shop. He does that all the time. He gives me work I can't do in the time I have. I'll just have to get started on it.

Dan and Kay Ramos go home at 5:00 when the shop closes. That is when I start painting the back.

I keep thinking about that call. I keep thinking about Ramos talking about me and my job.

I start looking at what is in the back. It's where the Ramoses work.

I go in the back of the shop. I start to clean a little. Ramos didn't say to clean there, but maybe I should.

Then I find this:

The two hot players on the Cougars' team are Will Cruz and Mack Day. Without Cruz and Day, the Cougars can't take the championship. What do you say?

I have a bad feeling. I forget the painting Ramos wants me to do. I get on my bike. I get out of there fast.

3. A Bad Feeling

I race home on my bike. I don't want to think. I don't want to see my little sisters. I don't want to be in my family. I want to be in Mack and Robin's family.

Mack doesn't know how good he has it. His family is like a TV family. They are one boy, one girl, and a happy mom and dad. They all smile. They talk at dinner. They go to the beach on Saturday. I can't believe it. They **like** each other.

My family is not like that. I have two little kid sisters. My mom and dad have problems. My dad drives a truck. Lots of nights he does not make it home. Then Mom says, "How can I raise three kids without a dad at home?"

He says back, "How can I raise three kids without a job? What do you want me to do?"

They go on and on. It makes me sick. I don't think they know if they like each other.

Then my mom says to me, "Keep that job, Will. If you don't, you will be driving a truck like your dad. I want you to go to college."

I don't like when she says that. I think driving a truck is OK. I think she says it to make my dad feel bad.

"I don't see **you** working. I don't see **you** going to college," Dad says to her.

Then Mom says to me, "I want more for you. You're a good boy. I want you to have more."

More? I think. More what?

Dad is not home when I get there after work. I have my dinner. I'm about to call Robin. She is Mack's sister. She and I go out. But when I start to make the call, Mom says, "Do your schoolwork. I don't want you going out."

"I **did** my work at school."

"All of it?"

"All of it."

"I want you home to help with your little sisters. Your dad will not be home."

"But Mom—"

"Don't talk back to me."

I'm at home all night. But Mom does not really need help. The little girls go to sleep after dinner. I think Mom just likes to have me home. She gets sick of being home without Dad all the time.

"Mom?" I say at about 10:00. "Did you call my boss?"

"No. I didn't need to."

"Just asking," I say.

Who called him to ask about me? I **know** Ramos was talking about me. Does he want to keep me working, or did he just want to ask me about Mack? I keep having that bad feeling.

At 10:30, Mom goes to sleep. I call Robin. After one ring, she says, "This is Robin."

"It's me," I say. Then I tell her about my day at Mountain Works. I tell her about hearing Ramos talk about me. I tell her about what I saw in the back of the shop.

"Do you think this is about you, Will? Just forget it. That call was not about you. Other people work there, you know."

"But what about the paper?" I ask. "**That** was about me."

Robin thinks. Then she says, "Should Dan and Kay Ramos be thinking about the Cougars' baseball team? Maybe he called some people when he gave you the job. Maybe he called Coach to see if you are a good kid. Maybe Coach wanted to talk Ramos out of giving you a job. I don't know! Just forget it, Will. I know you don't like Dan and Kay Ramos. But it's a good job. You make good money."

"OK, OK," I say, trying to forget it. "I'm just making it all up. I'll forget it."

"I think you should," Robin says.

I hear what she says. I don't know what to think, but I can't get away from that bad feeling.

4. The Ramos Kid

The next day at school I'm talking to Mack and Robin after class. Mack says, "We are in! We are going to the championships!"

"I'm happy for you," I say. I feel like throwing up.

"We will be playing the Dogs," he goes on. "They are a good team."

They are not really called the Dogs. That is what we call the team.

"You can do it," I say without any feeling. "No problem."

"You can come play with the team, you know," Mack says. "Coach wants you back on the team."

"I'm making money for college," I say. I'm trying to make him feel bad by talking about **money** and **college**.

Mack says, "You know what? Your boss's kid plays baseball for the Dogs."

"Are you kidding?" I say. "He didn't tell me that."

"They say that if he plays a good championship game, he will get big money to play college ball. He is the Dog's big hot player. He is really good."

I'm thinking hard. The Ramoses have not talked about having a kid who plays baseball. They know that I like baseball. I know that they didn't talk to me about the kid.

Robin says, "I hear that his mom and dad drive him. They just about don't give him time to sleep. It's baseball, baseball, baseball."

Mack says, "His dad has him working out at 6:00 a.m. Then he goes to school, and after that he works out with the team."

"This is college money," I say. "You think his mom and dad are driving him to get that."

"You have it," Mack says. "The Ramoses will do what it takes to get Tom—that is the Ramos kid—into the big time."

"I have to go," I say. I don't like what I'm hearing. I ride my bike home fast. I don't have to work that day.

I run in the house and scream, "Dad, are you home?"

"He is not home," Mom calls out. "What's going on?"

"May I call Dad?"

"He should be in the truck. You can call him on the CB."

I call Dad. "I have to talk to you," I tell him. "When are you coming home?"

"I'll be there by dinner," Dad says. I feel happy. I like it when Dad is home.

"Will you have time to talk?" I ask.

Dad laughs. "I'll have the time. If I can get away from your sisters and Mom."

"OK," I say. "I have to talk to you."

When Dad comes home that night, he has dinner. Then he puts on the TV. My little sisters jump all over him. After a long time, they go to sleep. Then Mom starts talking to Dad. I wait and wait and wait.

"Dad," I say. "I have to talk to you."

Mom looks at me.

18

"Man to man," I say. Dad looks at Mom. Mom gets up and goes to clean up after dinner. I tell him about the Ramos kid, Tom. Then I tell him about what Dan Ramos was saying. I tell him about the paper in the back of the shop.

The two hot players on the Cougars' team are Will Cruz and Mack Day. Without Cruz and Day, the Cougars can't take the championship. What do you say?

Then Dad says, "What do you think is going on?"

"Maybe I'm off the wall," I say. "But I think Kay and Dan Ramos gave me the job to keep me off the team. They know I'm a good baseball player. Tom Ramos will look good if I'm not playing. The idea is working. They are in the championships, and I'm not playing."

"Will, I think you have it. I don't think your idea is off the wall. What do you want to do about it?"

What? I'm used to Dad **telling,** not **asking** me what to do.

"I don't like being used," I say. "I want to play in that game. Coach keeps saying he wants me back on the team."

"Then that is what you should do."

"Really? But what about my job? What about making money?"

"You can get another job," Dad says. "I don't want you working for a man like that."

"Dad," I say, feeling happy, "are you going to be home for the game?"

"I want to be there," he says. "But I don't know. I'll see."

Then I don't feel that good anymore.

I think, **what good is the championship game if Dad is not going to be there?**

I'm making lots of money. If I keep the job, I can keep making money. I look at Dad, but he is going to sleep. I go help Mom clean up after dinner.

I don't know what I should do.

5. Giving Up the Job

I think it over for a long time. Dad may not come to the championship game. But I don't like the idea of the Ramoses having one over on me. I don't like being used. The more I think about it, the more mad I get.

I go to work the next day. I have it all worked out. I say to Dan and Kay Ramos, "I have some bad news. I have to stop working."

Dan Ramos is painting the wall in the back. It is the wall I had to stop painting. He stops and looks at me hard. "What are you talking about?"

I say, "You know that game next week?"

Kay is there. She says fast, "What about it?"

"I hear your kid, Tom, is playing."

Dan Ramos asks, "What about it?"

"I hear he is a good ballplayer."

"What are you getting at?" Kay Ramos walks up close to me. "Can't you work anymore?"

"I have another job," I say. I'm not making this up. Taking that championship **is** my job. The only job I want.

"Where?" she asks. "What job?"

"I can't say."

"Look," Ramos says. "I'll give you a raise. What do you want? $200 a week?"

I look at this man for a long time. Then I look at Kay Ramos. I think, **I'm happy I have my own mom and dad. My family has problems. But this family is sick!**

"I don't think I want more money," I say. "This new job I have, I'm doing it for my family."

"Then get out, if you don't want the work," Dan Ramos says. "I can find another kid. Get out."

I start to go. But I stop and say with a smile, "Good game next week. I'll be thinking of you."

I give a little wave, and I'm off.

6. Used No More!

Then I go see Coach at school. I'm not going to tell him about the Ramos kid. I don't like to tell on people. Who will believe me? Dan and Kay Ramos gave me a job. What of it? I was looking for a job for a long time. People all know that. People will not believe me about the Ramoses.

But it's not only knowing people will not believe me. I want to get back by playing this baseball game. I want to take that championship. I don't want the Ramoses problems to get in the way of our being the champions.

I say to Coach, "OK. I want back on the team if you will have me."

Coach looks at me for a long time. He says, "Just because we are playing in the big game? You know the other boys have been working long and hard. You're coming in for the good part."

"I know," I say. "I'm sorry. But I want to play if I can."

"OK," Coach smiles. "You know I want you back on the team. You will have to work really hard to make up for lost time."

"I can do that," I say. I'm mad.

The game is a week from Saturday. Coach works with me day after day. I hit and hit and hit. I hit the balls way out into the field. Mack throws with me at night. I can't wait. This will be a hot game.

I don't tell Mack about the Ramoses. I can just see him and Robin laughing. I can hear Robin saying, **"Do you think this is about you?"**

My dad is the only one I tell about the Ramoses. I'm happy I can talk to him. But I'm scared he will not come to the game. A part of me thinks we will take the championship **only** if my dad comes to the game.

7. Mack's Family

The game is in two days. The kids at school are all fired up. I can't believe I get to play. I can't wait to get back at the Ramoses for trying to use me—and my need for money—to take the championship.

Mrs. Hall, the principal, comes up to me at school. She says, "I hear you are going to play in the big game."

I look away. I think she wants to talk to me about college.

But she only smiles and says, "I'm happy to hear it. I'll be there."

"You will?" I say.

"I can't wait," she says. "The Cougars need a championship."

"Mrs. Hall?" I say. "I gave up my job to play on the team. I don't know if I can go to college anymore. I don't have the money."

Am I really saying this to her? What's my problem?

Mrs. Hall looks at me a long time. Then she asks, "Are you saying you don't **want** to go to college."

"No, I want to, but—" I start out.

She says, "Because I don't see you giving up that fast. One job is not going to stop you from what you want. I don't think it will. There are a lot more jobs out there. You can do what you want, Will. It's all up to you."

She walks off. What is it with Mom, Dad, and Mrs. Hall? They are all telling me I can do what I want. It feels good. I like thinking about what I want to do. I'm feeling happy.

After school, I go over to Mack's house. He is the only one home. "Where is Robin?" I ask.

"I don't know," he says. He looks bad.

"Where is your mom and dad?"

Mack looks out the window.

"What is it, Mack?" I say. "What's the problem?"

I can't believe he is looking this bad. After all, we are about to be playing some big time baseball. Mack and I will make this championship **real**.

Mack says, "My mom and dad can't, like, work it out."

"What!" I say. I don't get it. Mack and Robin's mom and dad are like the ones on TV. They smile at one another all the time. My family is the one with all the problems, I say, "I didn't think your family had any problems."

"Come off it," Mack says, getting mad. "All families have problems. But my family's problems are **big**. Dad went to my grandma's. He isn't coming to the game."

"I'm really sorry, Mack," I say. I know how he feels. If my dad doesn't come, I will feel bad.

"Maybe they will work it out by then."

"I don't think they will," Mack says. "It's over."

I say, "I didn't have any idea your family was having problems."

"In my family, we don't talk a lot," Mack says. "They don't tell **me** about the problems."

Mack looks like he is about to cry. I don't know what to do.

"Where is Robin?" I ask.

"I don't know!" Mack screams at me. "Stop talking to me!"

"OK, OK," I say. I'm going home. I don't know what I can do for Mack. "Call me if you need me."

I get on my bike and go home. I feel bad. People like to make problems for us kids all the time. I am sick of it. Mack is my friend. I don't want him feeling bad.

8. Robin Is Lost

At about 11:00 that night, I call Mack. When I get him, he asks, "Is that you, Robin?"

"Mack," I say, "it's me. What did you ask? Did you ask if I was Robin?"

"Will," he says, "do you know where Robin is?"

"She was in school."

"But she didn't come home," Mack says.

"Your mom and dad make her get in by 9:00 on school nights," I say.

"I know. But she has not called. Dad is at grandma's. Mom and I don't know where Robin is."

This is not good. It's not like Robin to make problems for her family.

"I'll come over," I say. "We have to go look for her."

"Go look **where**?"

"I don't know, Mack. But I want to come help you."

"OK," he says. "Mom will not stop crying. I don't know what to do."

"I'll be there fast."

My mom is sleeping. My dad is not home. I look in on my little sisters. They are OK. Then I take my mountain bike and go over to Mack's house.

"Do you know what she was wearing? What did you find in the house?"

"We looked all over the house. There is not a thing—not a paper—not a thing."

"Is her bike at home? Did she take the car?"

"Her bike is in the house. The car is out back."

"I think we should call the cops," I say. Mack does not like this idea. If we call the cops, it's like we are saying Robin is **really** lost.

"Can't we wait a little more?" he asks.

"We have to call the cops," I say. "We have to find her fast. They can help."

The cops come and ask us all about Robin.

Mack's mom tells the cops what is going on in the family.

One cop says, "I think she has run away. When a family has problems, kids run away."

"I don't know," I say. "Running away is not like Robin."

"We will look for her," the cop says. "Think of where she likes to go. Kids run away to friends or other family."

"We have called grandma's," Mack says. "She is not there."

"I don't think she has run away," I say one more time. But the cops don't hear me. They think they know. They talk more to Mack and Mack's mom. Then they go. They say they will try to find Robin.

I say to Mack, "The cops will try. But I think we should try on our own. Do you want to come with me?"

Mack says he does. "Will you be OK, Mom?" he asks.

"Go look," she says, "but be careful. Call me if you have **any** news."

"I will," Mack says, and we are off.

9. Did Robin Run Away?

We go on our mountain bikes to Donna's house. She is a good friend of Robin's. I don't want to get Donna's mom up. I hit lightly on what I think is Donna's window. But it's not. It's Donna's mom's window. She screams.

I call out, "It's OK! It's me, Will!"

Donna's mom looks out the window. "Do you know what time it is?" she calls out at us. She is really mad.

"I'm sorry," I say, "but we can't find Robin. Can I talk to Donna?"

"You can't find Robin? That's bad," Donna's mom says. "I'll get Donna."

Donna and her mom hear what we have to say. Then Donna says, "Robin was in class. But she didn't meet me after school. That is not like Robin. But I was just thinking she was with you, Will."

"She was not with me," I say. Then I ask, "Can you see Robin running away?"

"I can't," Donna says. "Robin doesn't run from problems. Ever. She knows how to work out her problems."

"You and she talk, don't you?" Donna's mom asks.

"We do. I just know Robin didn't run away. Robin is not going to run away without talking to me about it. I just know that."

Mack looks at me.

"That is what I think," I say. "I just don't see Robin, of all the girls I know, running away. It's not like her."

"Then **what**?" Mack asks.

"I don't know," I say. "We have to keep looking. We will tell you if we find her," I say to Donna. "Good night," I say to her mom. "Sorry we scared you."

Mack and I go back out into the night. We get on our bikes and go back to his house. "The game is on Saturday," I say.

"What game?" Mack asks.

"The **championship** game," I say. I don't want to stop talking about it. I don't want to give up on it. I don't think Robin is really lost. I think we can find her **and** play in the game.

"Forget the game," Mack says. I can tell he is in a bad way. He doesn't want to think about the championship game.

"Get some sleep," I say. "We will look for Robin after we get some sleep."

10. Hearing From Dan Ramos

The next day I'm about to go to school. It's one more day up to the time of the big game. My little sisters are running all over the house screaming. I can't think when they are doing that.

Then Mom says, "You have a call. I think it's Dan Ramos."

What does he want? I don't like the idea of him calling me. I don't work for him anymore.

I take the call.

Dan Ramos says, "I wanted to tell you that a girl, Robin Day, called you."

"What?" I say. "When?"

"You know I don't like you getting calls at work."

"I don't work for you anymore," I say. "What did she say?"

"Is she Mack Day's sister?" Dan Ramos wants to know.

What is he asking **that** for? I say, "Ramos, just tell me when she called. What did she say?"

"It was just a day ago. She wanted me to tell you she was going—. Where did she say she was going?"

"Think, Mr. Ramos," I say. "**Where**?"

He says, "She will be back. I don't think you have to get all fired up."

"She is not happy. Her mom and dad are having problems. Mack and I have to find her."

"Mack wants to find her?" Mr. Ramos asks.

What is the man's problem! Can't he help? Then I get that bad feeling, the one Dan Ramos gives me. I get the feeling he is fishing. He wants to know more about Mack's family.

I get mad. I say, "Tell me. Where did she say she was going?"

"The mountains, that's it. She was going up to Snow Pass."

"Did she say I should tell her mom and dad?" I ask. I'm trying to think out what Robin was doing.

"I don't know," Ramos says. "I have to go."

I think I get it. I think I know what Robin did. She was feeling bad about her mom and dad. She likes Snow Pass a lot. She goes there when she wants to think. It's not like her to go all night. But if she was feeling bad, maybe she did.

Robin doesn't know I stopped working at the Mountain Works shop. I think she wanted me to call her mom and Mack and tell them where she was going. I know that is it. We have to find her.

Next I call Mack. "I think I know where Robin is," I say. I tell him about Dan Ramos.

"There is a bus up there," Mack says. "We have to go look for her."

"No," I say. "We have to go to school." If we are not in school, we don't get to play in the championship game.

"I want to look for my sister," Mack says.

"You have to go to school," I say. "If you don't, they will take you out of the game."

"Forget the game," he says. "I have to find my sister."

"I'll get the car from Mom," I say. "We will go after school."

"Do we have time to wait?" Mack asks. "She was up there all night. I don't like that."

"She could sleep up there. She could be in a house."

"I don't know—" Mack says.

"We have to be in school," I tell him. "Mack, I have a feeling Robin is OK. She knows what she is doing."

"OK," he says. "We will go at 3:00."

I can't wait for the school day to be over. We don't have a team workout because of the big game the next day. Mack and I have to find Robin by night. If we don't, I know he will not play in the game.

Mom gives me the car after school. Mack and I take off for the mountains. We drive, and I tell Mack more about Dan Ramos. I tell him how it was hard to get Dan to tell me about Robin. Then I tell Mack about that other call and the paper. I tell him that I think Dan and Kay Ramos are trying to throw the championship game.

"You don't believe that!" Mack says. "We are just kids! They are not going to give you a job to keep you off the team. Get real, Will."

"What about that paper saying you and I are the hot players? That paper was in the back of his shop. Mack, what about how they drive the kid? What about the big college money they want him to get? If they get us out of the game, he is going to look real good."

Mack is thinking. "I don't know, Will," he says. "That is off the wall. After all, we are good. But we are not **that** good. Not like Tom Ramos. He is big time good."

"I know it's off the wall. But some people, like the Ramoses, **are** off the wall. Maybe the Ramoses want us off the team just to make the Ramoses kid look **good**."

"OK, OK," he says. "Maybe. But I can't think about the game. I just want to find my sister."

"I know," I say, hitting his back lightly. "We will find her."

11. Snow Pass

We drive up to Snow Pass. We get close, and I think about Robin. She likes to come to the mountains when she feels bad. But without a friend?

Mack and I get close to Snow Pass at 7:00 that night. It's snowing a little. What if she is out in this snow? What is she wearing?

I stop the car. Is this where Robin may be? We don't find her. We get to the top of the pass. I stop the car.

"We didn't find her," Mack says.

"I know about a little shelter up at the top," I say. "We can walk out to it. Maybe she is hiding there."

"In the snow?"

"Maybe." I say. "She was going to Snow Pass. This is the top of Snow Pass. We have to look."

We start walking out to the mountain shelter. I think Robin wanted me to call Mack and her Mom. But she didn't know I didn't work at Mountain Works anymore. Dan Ramos waited a day to say she called."

"It's not like Robin to go all night without telling Mom or me."

"Maybe the snow scared her. Maybe she is waiting in the shelter for the snow to stop."

"I don't know," Mack says. "I just don't see Robin taking the bus to the mountains."

"Do you want to go back, then? Go back home?"

"No. We have to look in the shelter at the top of the pass."

The snow is coming hard. I keep looking at the snow and the mountains. Did she have a sleeping bag? Is she cold? Where is she?

We get to the mountain shelter. "Robin!" I scream. "Robin! Are you in there?"

We hit on the wooden shelter. "Robin!" I call out. "Robin!"

Then I look in a window. It's dark in the shelter, but I can see she is not in there.

Mack has lost it. He is feeling bad. His sister is lost. It's snowing hard.

"She is not in there," I say. "We have to go back to the car. It's getting dark."

We start walking back to the car. The snow makes it hard to see where we walked coming in to the shelter.

"Where is the car?" Mack says. "I can't see."

The snow makes it dark out. We walk and walk, but we don't see the car.

"Where are we?" Mack asks. "Where is the car?"

"I don't know," I say. "I have lost the way."

"What should we do?" Mack wants to know.

"We have to go back to the shelter. We can wait in there for the snow to stop," I say. "Then we can find the car after it stops."

We go back to the shelter. The snow is coming harder. Mack and I are cold. I smash a window to get in the shelter. We go in.

I look at Mack, and he looks at me. I can see that our problems are only starting.

We get to the mountain shelter. "Robin!" I scream. "Robin! Are you in there?"

12. Sleeping in the Shelter

There is a lot of wood in the shelter. We make a big fire. The snow does not stop. It's getting dark.

The championship game is the next day. I can see that we will be in this shelter all night. We will not make it back for the game with all this snow.

But that is not the bad part. The bad part is: where is Robin?

Mack does not talk to me. After a long time, we go to sleep. The fire keeps us from getting cold.

The next day, I look out of the shelter. It's Saturday, the day of the big game. The snow has stopped.

I want to scream. How can it get this bad this fast? All I wanted was to have a job and play baseball. But we have lost Robin. I don't get to play in the game, and I don't have a job.

I get Mack up.

"Come on," I say. "I want to get out of the mountains."

Without the snow coming down, we can see. We find the car fast. I'm happy to be in the car. But Mack will not talk to me. He is mad we are up in the mountains.

"We have to call home," I say. We drive to a shop. I call home. I tell Mom about looking for Robin and having to sleep the night in the shelter. She is mad at me for going off. But she is happy I'm alive. Then Mack calls his mom. She didn't know he was not home. She is out of it, because of her problems with Mack's dad and Robin being away. She says Robin has not called.

We get back in the car. We start to drive back home. I think about the game. It starts at 5:00.

On the way home, Mack says, "Tell me one more time what you and Dan Ramos talked about—about where Robin was going."

Then Mack says, "Maybe he was making that up. I don't see Robin taking a **bus** to the mountains. Do you?"

"Yes, I think Dan Ramos is making it up." I say.

"To throw you and me off. To keep us from playing in the game."

"You're not saying he has taken Robin!"

"I'm not saying that. I think Robin did call him. But maybe Ramos was making up what she did say."

"Good thinking," I say. "After all, if the Ramoses gave me a job to keep me from playing baseball, maybe they are making up Robin's call. But then where **did** she go?"

"I have an idea," Mack says. "She looks after Mrs. Cook's kids. Mrs. Cook has a house at the beach. Maybe she went there. She is good friends with Mrs. Cook. She is like another mom to Robin."

"Mrs. Cook! We didn't think of that," I say.

"Because we believed Dan Ramos."

"Bad idea to ever believe him," I say. "Fast. To Mrs. Cook's beach house."

13. Getting Back

We get to Mrs. Cook's beach house at about 12:00. We drive in. Then we go up to the house. Mrs. Cook smiles at us. "What's up, boys?" she asks. Then she calls back into the house, "Robin, Mack and Will have come to see you!"

"Robin!" we call out.

"Mack! Will!" Robin says. She looks like she was crying. "What are you doing at the beach? What about the game?"

Mack and I look at one another. I feel so happy I'm about to pass out.

Mack says, "We have looked all over for you."

"You looked all over for me?" Robin asks. "I called Dan Ramos. He was going to tell you I went to Mrs. Cook's house at the beach all night. I asked him to tell Will to tell Mom and Mack. I needed some time away from home. Didn't he tell you, Will?"

"No," I say. "He didn't."

Mrs. Cook asks us to come in the house. We do. Then we tell Robin about Dan Ramos—that she was going up to the mountains and sleeping in the wooden shelter.

Robin gets mad. She says, "I **know** he didn't forget."

"I'll tell you what I think," Mack says. We tell Robin about my job. We talk about how the Ramoses want to make Tom look good on the baseball field.

"He is playing hardball," I say, feeling mad.

"What time is it?" Robin asks.

"Now it's 1:00."

"The game is at 5:00," she says. "How do you and Mack feel?"

"Feel? All I want is to sleep. I'm happy to see you, that is all."

"What Dan and Kay Ramos did to us is bad," Robin says. "They can't get away with that."

"No one will believe us," I say. "The call—the

paper—and the part about you—if I tell people about that, they will think I'm off the wall. Ramos can just say, 'I forget. The mountains, the beach, I don't know.'"

"He is not the only one who can play hardball," Robin says. "There is one way we can get back."

"What's that?" Mack wants to know.

"Take the championship game."

"How can we do that?" I say. "It's 1:00. Coach wants us on the field at 3:00."

"You can make it," Robin says. "Come on! Fast."

14. To the Game!

"Wait!" I say. I run out to the beach. I walk up to the sea. I look at the waves. I talk to the sea. I say I want it to work out with Robin and Mack's mom and dad. I want it to work out with my mom and dad. I want to take the championship game, too!

I run back to the car. Mack and Robin are waiting for me. We get in the car. Then we drive off. We get home at 2:30. I try to tell Mom about what is going on. But I have to talk fast. She makes me some dinner.

I'm about to race off to my game. Just then Dad walks in the house!

"Dad!" I scream out.

"It's the baseball champion," he says to me.

I laugh. "Are you coming to the game?"

"I didn't drive that truck that fast just to make it home for dinner," he says.

Then Mom smiles at him. I start to feel happy. I take off for the baseball field. Mack and Robin are meeting me there.

15. A Bad Start

Mack and I don't tell Coach what we have been doing. He doesn't ask. He is thinking only about the game.

He starts the team working out. We run the bases. Then we start throwing the ball. I need sleep. But that will not stop me from playing **hot** baseball.

It's just about 5:00. I see the Ramoses car drive up to the field. That makes me so mad I feel hot. I want to go over and tell the Ramoses what I think. But I hold back. We will get back by taking the championship.

There are a lot of people at the game. They are screaming, "Go Cougars! Smash the Dogs!" I look out and see my dad with my mom. My little sisters are running all over. In a way, I'm happy to see my little sisters and my mom and dad.

The game is about to start. Coach calls my team in off the field. We all run in. I see that the Ramoses are just in back of my team. I don't like that. I don't want the Ramoses hearing what Coach has to say.

"Coach," I say. Then Coach and I look back at the Ramoses. I say, "That Ramos kid. That is his mom and dad."

Coach looks mad. He says, "Mrs. Ramos, go by your own team."

I see Dan and Kay Ramos smile. Then Dan Ramos sees me. I can see that he is mad I'm playing. All that money he put into me and my job. But that didn't stop me from playing in the game after all. That is what they get for trying to throw the game!

Coach keeps looking at the Ramoses. They get up and walk over to be in back of the other team.

Then Coach gives us a good talking to. He says to play hard. We run out on the field. I can hear all the kids from my school screaming. I can hear Mrs. Hall calling out, "Go, Cougars!" Then the school band starts playing. I feel good.

I look out at Mack in the field. Robin is the only one in his family at the game. I know he is not feeling happy. But he is being big. He is playing the championship game for the team.

The Dogs are up. They start out smashing the ball. They get three hits—1, 2, 3 on base.

"Stop the Dogs!" I hear Dad scream.

"Stop the Dogs!" My little sisters scream like my dad.

Then the Ramos kid is up. He hits the ball hard. He hits the ball out of the ball field. All four boys run home. The game has only started, and it's 0 to 4. I feel sick.

The next kid hits a ball to me. I throw him out. Then Mack gets the next out in the field. We need one more out. I wait for the ball to come to me another time.

But the next one goes out in the field. The kid gets a run. Then the next two kids get hits. A big kid is up. If he hits the other kids in, the game is all over. It will be 0 to 5. The big kid smashes the ball. It goes way out in the field. Mack runs and runs. He gets it!

We all run in off the field. Mack is smiling. I hit him on the back.

Now we are up.

16. The Home Run

We get one out. Then we get another out. I'm up. I look up and see Dan and Kay Ramos looking at me. They are smiling. They think they have the championship. I wait for the ball. It comes. I try to hit it, but I don't.

But then I hit the next ball that comes to me. It goes way out in the field. I take off running. But the Ramos kid gets my hit. He throws me out.

The Dogs are up. I feel bad. I can hear my little sisters screaming for me. I look up. "Go, Will!" they call out. I have to smile. Mom waves at me. I think maybe I'm not that good at baseball. But I like my family a lot more than the Ramoses.

Coach calls out, "OK, Cougars, one-two-three outs. Make it fast."

In no time, we are back up. This time we do

OK. We get some hits. But we do not get any runs. There are no outs.

Then I get up. There is one boy on base. I hit the ball. It goes way out in the field. I start to run. I hear people screaming. Then I hear my dad scream. That makes me go faster. I don't look out in the field. I wait to hear what Coach says. I can hear him saying, "Keep going! Keep going!"

Then I'm running home. I hear Coach scream, "Way to go, Will."

I can't believe I hit a home run!

It's 2 to 5. No outs. Mack goes up to hit. He smashes one out in the field. The next player smashes another one. Then we get two outs.

The next player hits in one run. It's 3 to 5. Then we get another out.

We run back out to the field. We are in this game after all! It's going to be close. But I know what I want. I want to take this championship.

17. Champions

The Dogs get another run. It's 3 to 6. But when we are up, we get two fast runs. That makes it 5 to 6. It's Cougars, 5 to Dogs, 6. It's that way for a long time. The game is just about over. The Dogs have no more ups.

We are up. I can hear Dan Ramos calling out, "Hold the Cougars! Hold the Cougars!"

People are screaming. No one can believe we are doing this good with the Dogs. They are a good team. All we need is two runs. Can we do it?

I look at the Dogs in the field. They think they can hold us.

We get two outs fast. I want to throw up. Then I'm up. I look at one ball go by. Then I look at the next one.

"Make it be good!" Coach is screaming. "Wait for the good one."

I get walked. Next Mack is up. I start talking, "Come on, Mack. You can do it. Come on, Mack."

But I know Mack is not feeling good. His dad didn't make it to the game. His mom didn't make it to the game. **Mack** is only at the game because I wanted him to come.

I hear Dan Ramos call out, "This kid can't hit! The game is over. One more out! Go get him, Dogs!"

Mack is waiting for the ball. I can see him stop and look at Dan Ramos. Then I see him get fired up. Maybe he is thinking about what Dan and Kay Ramos did to his sister.

The ball comes at him. Mack smashes the ball. It goes, and it goes, and it goes. The ball is out of the field. I run the bases. Mack runs after me.

Mack and I come running into home. We have the championship! 7 to 6. The Cougars are the champions!

People are screaming. My little sisters find me. They are all over me. My mom and dad find me. I have not been this happy. Ever.

Then I see Dan and Kay Ramos. I go over, and I say, "I know what you wanted to do by giving me that job. I know you didn't tell me where Robin was just to throw Mack and me off our game. It didn't work. We have the championship." Then I walked away.

We have the championship.

18. Dad's New Job

That night my dad asks Coach and the team to come over to our house. We talk all about the game. We play a lot of CDs. We have a good time. We are happy. We are the champions.

After a long time, people go home. Mack and Robin talk a long time with my family.

Dad says, "I have some good news."

"What?" I say.

"I have a new job. I'll be running the new car and truck parts shop. The money is good. I'll be home all the time."

I look at Mom. She is smiling big.

"I'll be home night after night," Dad says, laughing. "I'll drive your mom up the wall."

We all laugh with him. Then I look at Mack and

Robin and feel bad. I'm **not** the one with family problems!

Robin knows what I'm thinking. "It's OK," she says. "I'm happy to see that some families can work it out." She looks at Mack. "I think Mom and Dad will. It takes time."

"That it does," my dad says. "It takes time."

I get this big feeling in me. I'm happy to have friends like Robin and Mack. But most of all, I'm happy to have my family.